Foucault in Tahrir Square

Discourse Analysis and The Social Construction of Crowd

Shady Lewis

Abstract

The way in which the crowd is constructed has been shown to be the site of power struggles between the status quo and political change. However, there is little qualitative research on how crowd members construct their experiences of participation in crowd activity. This study examines how the crowd in the Tahrir square sit-in during the 2011 Egyptian revolution was constructed by crowd members themselves. Based on semi-structured interviews with five Egyptian demonstrators regarding their experiences of this sit-in, a Foucauldian discourse analysis indicated that crowd members were subject to a set of discourses that served to normalise or problematise the crowd by constructing its processes as either compatible or problematic compared with the values of the neoliberal agenda respectively. Drawing on Foucault's ideas on governmentality, the discursive repertoires available to crowd members were shown to regulate the ways in which they constructed their subjectivity and social action, governing their conduct in line with the neoliberal ideal of the autonomous, responsible individual. It was shown that in constructing crowd self-regulatory practices, crowd members legitimised or resisted techniques of social control internal to the crowd that limited their ability to bring about political change. Possible recommendations for crowd activism and implications for research are discussed.

Table of Contents

3.   Analysis and Discussion

3.1.   Subjectification in the crowd

3.1.1.   The crowd and rationality

3.1.2.   The crowd and experience

3.1.3.   The crowd and senses of safety and danger

3.1.4.   The crowd and risk taking

3.2.   The crowd as warranting social action

3.2.1.   The crowd and self-regulation

3.2.2.   The crowd and gender

3.2.3.   The crowd and violence

4.   Conclusion and critique

4.1. Revisiting research aims, key analytical foci and recommendations

4.2.   Evaluation and implications

References

Introduction

This project explores how the crowd is constructed by those who take part in crowd action themselves. In this case, the crowd members were the demonstrators who participated in the Tahrir Square sit-in (from 28 December 2010 to 11 February 2011) during the 2011 Egyptian revolution. This fifteen-day-long sit-in not only forced Egyptian president Mubarak from power, thereby ending his thirty years of oppressive rule, but also inspired the Arab Spring, a revolutionary wave of civil uprisings that erupted across the region (2010-ongoing), as well as the Occupy Movement, a wider international protest movement against social and economic injustice (2011-ongoing). Having been involved in Egyptian protest movements for the last ten years, I am personally interested in exploring the behaviours and processes of crowd members and the crowd as a whole to gain more understanding regarding the role of crowds in challenging political oppression and social injustice. I am particularly interested in exploring this topic from the under-researched perspective of the crowd members themselves.

Because crowds have been able to bring about sudden, dramatic and radical political change, in a way that has bypassed established due processes and has threatened the status quo, they have provoked controversy historically. On one hand, crowds empower ordinary people, especially the oppressed, to gain direct power by acting collectively to overturn or challenge oppression and inequalities (Van

Zomeren & Speers, 2011). On the other hand, government and the agencies responsible for crowd management perceive crowds as a potential risk to public safety and order (Cronin & Reicher, 2006). In this context, the Egyptian state-owned media has portrayed the Tahrir Square sit-in crowd as destructive, irrational, barbaric and chaotic, whereas the independent Egyptian and Western media have described it as spontaneous, rational, well-organised and civilised (Fornaciari, 2012; Khamis, 2011).

The current research explores some of these claims by examining how the Tahrir Square crowd members made sense of their experiences in the sit-in. This research utilises a social constructionist epistemology, which does not take our experiences of the world and ourselves at face value (Burr, 1995) but situates people's constructions of their experiences within their social and historical contexts and considers them to serve a range of interpersonal and societal functions (Harper, 2012). From a critical realist perspective, the limitations and possibilities that are inherent in the material world and its social structures shape and constrain these discursive constructions (Parker, 1992). Drawing on Foucault's ideas of knowledge, power, resistance and governmentality as well as the work of Rose (1999) and McNay (2009) concerning the autonomous individual as the product of neoliberalism and Western psychology, it is my thesis that the crowd members of this study are subject to a set of wider societal discourses that normalise certain crowd activities and problematise others. These discourses serve either as means of social control or resistance with regard to the power struggles between the status quo and political change. The analysis in this study demonstrates how the discursive repertoires available to participants served to regulate the ways in which they constructed the crowd and themselves and governed their conduct in line with the neoliberal agenda.

This introduction first evaluates how psychology has understood the crowd to date. It subsequently proceeds to examine the existing research on crowds before presenting an alternative understanding of the crowd based on social constructionist ideas.

1.1. Psychology's understanding of the crowd: A critical reflection

1.1.1. Classic theories of the crowd

This section briefly introduces classic theories of the crowd and how mainstream psychology has problematised them. In the nineteenth century, crowd psychology emerged as a response to the social control crisis linked to the formation of a mass rural working class and the political unrest caused by the ability of the working class crowds to overthrow political regimes and threaten social order (Reicher, 1987). In this context, Le Bon (1895), who witnessed the wave of European revolutions in 1884 as a child, wrote his influential book "The Crowd: A study of the popular mind". In this book, Le Bon proposed that

people lose their individual identities, their sense of responsibility
and self-control within a crowd and become subject to contagion and
suggestibility. As a result, behaviour within a crowd is dominated by
what Le Bon referred to as "racial unconscious" or "group mind",
which is characterised by emotionality, irrationality, impulsivity and
irritability. Le Bon's group mind theory not only played a crucial role in
shaping the classic image of the crowd but also formed the basis for the
later de-individuation theories that describe the process through which
people lose their individual identities and engage in unrestrained,
impulsive and anti-social behaviours within a crowd (Diener 1979;
Festinger, Pepitone & Newcomb, 1952; Singer, Brush & Lublin, 1965).

Stott, Hutchison and Drury (2001) argued that these deindividuation
theories were first challenged by Allport's (1924) pre-disposition
theory. Allport proposed that collective behaviour is not the result of
group mind or racial unconscious but the result of similarities among
the pre-existing individual tendencies of crowd members. He also
believed that social facilitation within a crowd reveals the instinct of
struggle (i.e., the tendency to destroy anything that prevents the
satisfaction of one's basic needs; Reicher, 2001). Contrary to the
deindividuation theories that attributed crowd processes to the
collective nature of the crowd, the predisposition theory attributed
crowd processes to the individual characteristics of its members.
Despite the differences between these accounts, they share two basic
assumptions: crowd behaviour is inevitably destructive and a

manifestation of universal characteristics (Reicher, 1987). These assumptions strongly influenced not only thoughts and research in Social Psychology, but also popular culture (Drury, Cooking & Reicher, 2009), Sociology introductory texts (Schweingruber & Wohlstein, 2005), public order policing (Cronin & Reicher, 2006), military thoughts (Bendersky, 2007), design of public places (Drury & Winter, 2003) and judicial decisions (Colman, 1991) for many years.

In the last three decades, however, mainstream psychology has problematised these classic models at various levels. First, these models, which claimed scientific validity, were criticised for lacking empirical evidence. For example, a meta-analysis of sixty deindividuation studies did not find evidence to support the deindividuation theory (Postmes & Spears, 1998). Furthermore, empirical evidence showed that crowd violence is rare (Schweingruber & Wohlstein, 2005). Other studies on crowd behaviour in emergencies demonstrated that crowd members do not show irrationality; rather, they show solidarity, mutual cooperation and coordination (e.g., Drury, Cocking & Reicher, 2009; Drury & Winter, 2003).

Second, the classic theories of the crowd were criticised for isolating the crowd from its contexts and separating the individual from the social; hence, these theories missed the full complexity of crowd activity (McPhail, 1991; Nye, 1975; Reicher, 1987; Reicher & Potter 1985). The classic models assumed that crowd actions are not rational and do not pursue meaningful goals within a social and historical context; rather, they are irrational actions determined by universal and invariant features of the crowd or its members. In this sense, the classic models were overly deterministic because they viewed the crowd as inevitably pathological and destructive regardless of the type of the gathering, its goals, the ideologies of those involved, or the role of authorities in crowd events.

Third, the classic theories of the crowd that claimed scientific objectivity and neutrality were criticised for being politically motivated and ideologically biased (Reicher, 1987; 2001). These theories were a systematic manifestation of the hostility of the ruling class and traditional social institutions towards the working-class crowds and the threat they posed to the social order (Bendersky, 2007). Therefore, classic theories were not interested in understanding crowd phenomena but in providing a scientific justification for the ruling class's view of crowds as undesirable and destructive, thereby discrediting crowds and legitimising the suppressive practices of social control that aim to eliminate them (Drury, 2003).

1.1.2. Societal theories of the crowd and contemporary research

The Emergent Norm Theory (Turner & Killian, 1987) first challenged the predisposition theory (Allport, 1924). The Emergent Norm Theory proposed that crowd processes are governed by social norms that emerge in the crowd event itself. These norms are formed through group interactions during a period of milling that precedes crowd action. However, this theory failed to explain how social norms can change rapidly in crowd events where there is little time for milling (McPhail, 1991). Moreover, although this theory viewed crowd norms as a product of intra-group interactions, it remained overly reductionist and individualistic in assuming that these norms are determined by the predispositions of the individuals within the crowd (Reicher, 1996).

The development of the social identity model of crowd behaviour, which was based on self-categorisation theory (Turner, Oakes, Haslam & McGarty, 1994), was the next major step towards explaining crowd phenomena on a societal level. The social identity model (Reicher, 1984; 1987) proposed that crowd members identify themselves as members of a social category and then act in terms of this contextually specified common identity. Constructing this social identity involves a stereotyping process whereby crowd members form and seek to conform to norms that define a shared category. Pre-existing categories, cultural values, and ideologies, as well as social and historical contexts in general, determine the development of these stereotyped norms.

To address the dynamic interplay between the groups involved in crowd events, Reicher (1996; 1997) developed the Elaborated Social Identity Model (ESIM). This model placed greater emphasis on the fact that crowd events are usually inter-group encounters (e.g., the police vs. demonstrators). The ESIM viewed social identity as a model of self in relation to other groups and assumed that the actions of other groups partially construct the context of crowd events. Therefore, this model viewed inter-group dynamics as crucial to social identity formation and crowd processes (Doosje, Spears & Ellemers, 2002; Drury & Reicher, 1999). The ESIM also acknowledged the importance of intra-group dynamics in the process whereby crowd members make sense of their social identities (Drury & Reicher, 2000).

Drury (2003) argued that the societal theories, which consider crowd actions as meaningful and both enabled and limited by a shared identity, contribute to the ideological struggle against classic theories of the crowd; hence, they normalise the crowd and delegitimise the repressive practices of crowd control. However, Durrheim and Foster (1999) argued that the societal theories that view crowds as relational and self-regulated provide the ontological and epistemological conditions of possibility for the liberal-democratic forms of crowd management that seek to manage crowds through authority internal to them by strategies aimed at intensifying self-regulatory processes. Whereas the development of a practical crowd control policy based on classic theories that consider crowds to be inevitably irrational and destructive is highly problematic in liberal-democratic societies, societal theories have offered a scientific basis from which to develop and institutionalise regulatory processes of crowd control that are ideally suited to these societies. This argument will be further discussed in Section 1.3.

Recently, a body of literature on different types of crowds has accumulated that has situated crowds in their historical, social and cultural contexts. However, the majority of mainstream literature on the crowd is descriptive and observational. Therefore, it is positivist and characterised by the Cartesian dualism that locates crowd members within their individual traits, motivations, emotions, and cognitions or in relation to social factors such as crowd demographics and hierarchy. These factors are understood to exist within a single objective reality, isolating the social construction of the crowd from its wider historical, cultural, political and economic conditions.

Although there is some literature on the relationships between crowd action, change and empowerment (Drury, 2002; Drury & Reicher, 2005), the majority of studies have been concerned with understanding the factors that influence crowd behaviour in situations of public disorder, such as football hooliganism (Stott, Adang, Livingstone & Schreiber, 2008), riots (Vider, 2004) and mass emergencies (Rogesch, Schreckenberg, Tribble, Kingsch & Kretz, 2008). These studies have aimed to provide a psychological basis for crowd control models that minimise the risks that crowds pose to public order and maximise public safety. Much of this literature has focused on crowd events in Western countries, except for a few studies that have been concerned with crowd management in disaster situations in developing countries (Ammar, 2007).

Little qualitative research exists that directly focuses on crowd members' experiences of crowd events (e.g., the individual experiences of solidarity among members of mass emergency events; Drury, Cooking & Reicher, 2009). Much of this research has concluded that these experiences can be understood as the product of intra- and inter-group dynamics as well as the shared identity that these crowd members acquire. However, only a few discursive studies have examined crowd members' accounts of crowd events. Drury (2002) presented a critical discursive analysis of newspaper accounts of an "anti-paedophile" crowd action that occurred in the UK in 2000. This study outlined the rhetorical and ideological functions of the constructions of the crowd identified in newspapers, including those offered by crowd members themselves. However, beyond this, little research has examined how people make sense of their experiences in crowd events, which makes this an area worthy of further examination.

1.3.   An alternative understanding of the crowd: The constructionist perspective

The previous sections evaluated mainstream psychology's understanding of the crowd. This section outlines an alternative way to understand the crowd. Specifically, I will argue that Foucault's ideas on governmentality, as well as Rose's (1999) and McNay's (2009) ideas on the construction of the neoliberal subject, provide a useful framework to examine how individuals' accounts of crowd events are discursively produced and regulated.

1.3.1.   Foucault, governmentality and the crowd

Foucault introduced the notion of governmentality to explain the "autonomous" individual's capacity for self-control and how this capacity is linked to modern forms of political rule and economic structures (McNay, 2009). Therefore, this notion is a useful tool to explore the ways in which crowds might be regulated by practices of social control in modern societies.

In his earlier works, Foucault argued that power in the modern era is exercised, not only through repressive means but also through "disciplinary powers" by which modern states govern their populations and maintain social control. These powers are exercised through different means: through the designs of prisons, schools and hospitals that render the individual constantly visible to the state's disciplinary

gaze which normalises and privileges certain practices and penalises
and pathologises others and hence fosters forms of self-discipline;
through scientific disciplines such as psychology, sociology and
criminology that create measurements and descriptions of "normal"
individuals and their conduct, which produce a population of "useful
and docile bodies"; and through various techniques of surveillance,
normalising judgement and examination at the level of institutions
(Foucault, 1972; 1982).

In this context, crowds in modern societies are not only controlled
through the oppressive power of police forces but also through subtle
forms of social control and disciplinary practices. These practices
include the legal codes and procedures that regulate political protests
and public order; health and safety procedures for crowd events; and the
design of public areas that are based on the psychological knowledge
that normalises certain types of crowds and problematises others.
Furthermore, the police, CCTV systems, health and safety officers for
crowd events, and the bureaucratic institutions responsible for issuing
permissions for public protests are part of the state's disciplinary gaze.
These disciplinary practices which are used to control crowds, are
similar to the devices in prisons that Foucault (1977) described as
meant to abolish the crowd conceived as "a compact mass, a locus of
multiple exchanges, individualities merging together, a collective
effect" and replace it with "a collection of separate individualities";

hence, "to induce in the inmate a state of conscious and permanent visibility that assures the automatic functioning of power" (p. 201).

Foucault later developed the notion of "governmentality" to link the concept of "technologies of power", which seek to control social conduct at the institutional level, with the concept of "technologies of self", through which individuals come to regulate their own conduct "with regard to the true and false, the permitted and the forbidden and the desirable and the undesirable" (Foucault, 1988, p. 144). Foucault viewed the human subject as constituted by discursive practices that operate within "regimes of truths", in the form of discourses about human psychology, religion, gender, ethnicity and culture. Discursive practices produce permitted identities or subjectivities as well as the permitted actions for the object of a discourse. These practices are not commands from a higher authority but operate by individualising the human subjects, attaching them to their own identities and imposing a law of truth that they and others must recognise in them (Foucault, 1982).

Durrheim and Foster (1999) utilised this Foucauldian framework to analyse the South African Regulation of the Gatherings Act of 1993 and argued that crowds raise political dilemmas for liberal governments. On one hand, freedom of expression and association which are the core values of liberal democracy should be seen to be permitted and preserved by the state. On the other hand, crowds are threats to liberal democratic states because their radical powers pose a risk to the status quo. Liberal governments solve this dilemma by governing "at a distance" by subjecting crowds to "technologies of power" and "technologies of self" that enable processes of crowd self-regulation whereby the autonomous and free subjects may be regulated by means of their autonomy and responsibility. For example, the South African Regulation of Gathering Act of 1993 legalises an organisational hierarchy within the crowd - the protest organizers who mediate between the crowd and the police - and institutionalises a set of practices aimed at them such as negotiations, setting timetables and issuing permits to ensure that the crowd remains peaceful.

This act not only institutionalises an internal surveillance system within the crowd but also normalises "the peaceful crowd" as a feature of democratic society. This discourse of "peace" divides the legitimate and peaceful crowd from the illegitimate and violent crowd, thereby establishing an ethical hierarchy through which to understand varieties within both crowds and individuals. The discourse of "peace" actively produces permitted subjectivities and actions through which crowd members regulate their own conduct.

Therefore, governmentality is a useful lens whereby to examine the ways crowd members are subject to the "technologies of power" and "technologies of self" that shape their subjectivities and regulate their conduct in line with the dominant discourses in their society. The next section explains how contemporary societal structures have produced a certain kind of subjectivity – that of the neoliberal individual – which is relevant to the ways in which individuals understand themselves and their experiences as well as how they govern their own conduct within crowd events.

1.3.2.   The construction of the neoliberal individual

Drawing on Foucault's notion of governmentality, McNay (2009) argued that the central principle of governmental control in neoliberal societies is the organisation of all social relationships around the notion of enterprise. The generalisation of the enterprise form is so exhaustive that it is not only confined to social relations but intended to encompass subjectivity itself. Individuals are encouraged to view themselves as an individual enterprise, responsible for managing their own lives and a "diverse network" of enterprises such as "work, household, pension, insurance, and private property" in a way that enables them to avoid risk and maximise their happiness (McNay, 2009, p. 61). Individual autonomy is not the limit of the neoliberal form of social control, but it is one of the central technologies that operate in the context of a notion of responsible self-management. This construction of the self normalises certain understandings of ourselves, identities, and experiences as well as the possibilities for social actions available to us.

Rose (1999) argued that the Western "Psy disciplines", which include psychology, have played a central role in normalising and privileging the construction of the autonomous, responsible and governable individual. These disciplines are seen as productive of true knowledge about human nature based on scientific expertise that normalises certain subjectivities and pathologises others. In this context, classic theories of the crowd such as Le Bon's have problematised crowds by construing them as a threat to the individuality, rationality and autonomy of its members. On the other hand, recent theories in crowd psychology (Reicher, 1996; 1997) have construed crowd members in line with neoliberal values as autonomous individuals with the capacity for rational decision-making who manage their conduct according to their shared identity. Thus, the crowd is constructed in two contradictory accounts in relation to neoliberal values, which might have significant implications for how crowd members make sense of themselves and their experiences, and the possibilities for actions available to them.

1.3.3.   The neoliberal individual and the Egyptian citizen

How is the notion of the neoliberal subject relevant to the Egyptian citizens in this study? Egypt is hardly a post-industrial society, and it has only recently become a democracy. However, under Anwar Sadat and Hosni Mubarak (1970-2011), the aggressive neoliberal economic policies that sought to privatise public resources and encourage market entrepreneurship exposed Egyptian citizens to globalised, free-market values. This exposure coincided with the emergence of a neoliberal narrative of free markets and personal autonomy that dictated a new relationship between the citizens and the state over the last forty years. Recent studies have shown how the neoliberal ethical agenda has been dominant in shaping subjectivities and social relationships in Egypt including political subjectivities of Egyptian citizens (Ismail, 2011); the narrative of freedom and autonomy in artwork and practices of Egyptian visual artists (Schindler, 2012); the Muslim self in Islamic youth organisations as characterised by personal responsibility, individual initiative, and a focus on projects and goals (Harris, 2010); and certain forms of care and responsibility that emphasise neo-liberal values such as freedom and entrepreneurship at international schools in Cairo (Caldwell, 2012).

Above all, the crowd in this study which took to the streets of Egypt demanding political changes that included free elections, a liberal constitution and a representative democracy was inspired by the values of Western liberal democracy. Some have argued that the 2011 Egyptian revolution was a revolt against the failure of neoliberal economic policies paired with authoritarianism (Joya, 2011). However, participants in the Egyptian revolution demanded political changes that are in line with the neoliberal agenda: personal freedom, autonomy and responsibility. In this sense, one can argue that the crowd of Tahrir Square revolted against neoliberal economic policies but within the neoliberal framework of values that shaped their subjectivity and social action.

1.4. Research questions

The above introduction demonstrates that a constructionist study on crowd members' accounts of their experiences in crowd events, which examines how they constructed the crowd, their interactions within it, and themselves as crowd members, is warranted. In seeking to address this, the current research considers the subject positions which these constructions enable and the implications of various subject positions for social action. It seeks to identify the ways in which crowd members construct themselves as subject to the processes of governmentality, at the levels of both the individual and the institution. It also examines evidence of resistance within the crowd members' talk.

Therefore, the following analysis and discussion seeks to answer the following questions:

1.4.1. Main research question

How do the Egyptian demonstrators who participated in the Tahrir square sit-in construct the crowd with regard to this experience?

1.4.2. Secondary research questions

How do these constructions serve to normalise, problematise or privilege the crowd?

What subject positions are enabled by these constructions, and what are the implications for action of these subject positions, particularly with regard to crowd action?

How are crowd members subject to the practices of governmentality at the level of the crowd (disciplinary power) and the level of the individual (self-regulation)?

2. Method

2.1. Recruitment and participants

This study aimed to recruit between eight and ten participants who lived in Egypt and had diverse life experiences and backgrounds in order to gain a wide spectrum of discursive repertoires. However, due to the ethical reasons explained in Section 2.3, the interviews were not conducted in Egypt; rather, Egyptian participants who lived in the UK were recruited.

Five participants were recruited through an action group that works with the Egyptian community in the UK. With permission from this action group, an information leaflet was sent to all of the registered group members on its mailing list. Eight people contacted me to express their interest in participation. However, only five of them attended the interviews. All participants were Egyptian citizens who took part in the Tahrir Square sit-in during the 2011 Egyptian Revolution. However, they resided in the UK when these interviews were conducted. The participants were aged between 24-33 years and included four women and one man. All participants were post-graduate social science students who were granted scholarships from British universities, except for one participant who had been living and working in the UK for the last ten years. All participants identified themselves as single and belonging to the Egyptian middle class.

2.2.   Reflexivity

According to Willig (2008), there are two types of reflexivity: personal and epistemological. The latter of these types is discussed in Section 4, whereas the issue of personal reflexivity is addressed in this section. Specifically, I reflect on the ways that my own identities, experiences, values, beliefs and interests might have shaped this research. Moreover, I explore the dynamics of the researcher-participant relationship and how it might have influenced this research. As an Egyptian citizen who was a member of the Egyptian Movement for Change, a political group that has put forward crowd action as the only means for Egyptian political change since 2006, I am aware that the topic has a personal resonance for me. I began this project seeking to acknowledge the role that crowds play in acquiring political change and explore the experiences of those who participated in the Tahrir square sit-in. However, I later adopted a critical realist perspective (Parker, 1992) that was not concerned with revealing universal truths about the crowd but was interested in exploring the ways in which participants construct the crowd and how these constructions might be the site of power struggles between the status quo and political change.

I am also aware that, being like most of the participants in this project, a member of the Egyptian middle class that Western values have heavily influenced has shaped this project at every stage, including developing the research questions and collecting, selecting and interpreting the data. However, this should not be seen as a problem but as an opportunity (Finlay, 2002) to explore the discursive resources deployed in the accounts of this particular social group that played a major role in the 2011 Egyptian Revolution. In this sense, I am aware of my role as a researcher in the (co)-construction of knowledge in collaboration with the participants (Willig, 2008).

In line with social constructionist practice, I considered the power relationship within the interview encounter (Parker, 1992). I tried to address power inequalities between the participants and myself as the researcher (and therefore "expert") by making clear to the participants that the aim of the project was not to psychologically analyse them and emphasising that they were more knowledgeable than me with regard to the topic because I did not participate in the Tahrir Square sit-in. I also employed co-authorship (Kvale, 1996) by inviting participants to introduce topics that they felt were important during the interviews.

2.3. Analytic method

This project employed a Foucauldian discourse analysis (FDA). This analytic method is grounded in a critical realist epistemological framework, which theorises that the limitations and possibilities inherent in the material world and its social structures shape and constrain discursive constructions (Parker, 1992). Therefore, I situated my analysis within the material conditions of possibilities, being aware of how Egyptian political and social structures and factors such as education, social class, political affiliations and the availability of resources might influence the ways in which participants deploy discursive resources.

Although there are no precise methodological principles with set rules and procedures associated with FDA (Arribas-Ayllon & Walkerdine, 2008), this analytic method is mainly characterised by utilising Foucault's (1972) theorisation of the constitutive properties of language and his conception of knowledge as socially constructed in discourses that do not simply reflect reality but rather construct certain ways-of-seeing the world and certain ways-of-being in the world (Willig, 2008). It also draws on Foucault's (1977) ideas regarding the role of discourses in the wider social processes of legitimation and power, specifically in the ways that they promote certain knowledges as "true" and make available certain subjectivities and social actions through which relations of power are realised. Therefore, my analysis was concerned with examining the ways in which participants used the discursive resources available to them to construct the crowd and their experiences of participation in crowd activities as well as legitimatise certain subject positions and social practices within this context. Because Foucault (1990, p. 95) once stated that "where there is power, there is resistance", my analysis examined the ways in which resistance functions within the discourses of the crowd and how resistance can function to strengthen the same dominant discourses it tries to challenge (Harper, 1995). I also drew on Foucault's idea of governmentality (McNay, 2009; Rose, 1999) to explore how the ways in which participants deployed various discursive resources were linked to technologies of power, technologies of self and neoliberal values.

2.5.   Analytic Process

Step 1

The interviews were transcribed into a table, and notes regarding the objects being constructed, subjectivity and social actions were recorded in a specific column. Ideas and comments regarding connection to the literature and Foucault's ideas concerning governmentality were recorded in another column. The transcript of each interview was read three times in different sequences (Participants 1 through 5, Participants 5 through 1 and in a random order) to ensure that the analysis was not primed by the first interview(s).

Step 2

The constructed objects, events and experiences (e.g., the crowd as "rational" or "irrational" and so on) were listed and mapped out for each interview by drawing arrows between areas that were linked in the participants' talk. Ideas regarding the secondary questions concerning subjectivity and social actions enabled by these constructions and processes of governmentality were recorded.

Step 3

A list of the key constructs in the text that were relevant to the research   questions was created. These constructs included the contradictory accounts of the crowd or challenges to these accounts. Based on this list, two primary analytic foci were identified to address the research questions: constructions of the crowd that allow subjectification and constructions of the crowd that warranty social actions.

Step 4

Decisions regarding which constructions to include were based on whether the extracts within and between interviews supported them. Specific extracts were chosen to exemplify these constructions. These extracts were then contrasted and linked together in a way that attempted to provide a narrative of how participants constructed their experiences of the crowd activity.

Step 5

Drawing on the notes and maps from the above four stages, the analysis was written up in a more comprehensive way adding links to the relevant literature. The analysis was then refined to provide overall coherence.

3.   Analysis and Discussion

The following analysis presents the demonstrators' constructions of the crowd in relation to their experience of participation in the Tahrir square sit-in during the Egyptian Revolution. These constructions are presented in two sections: First, how participants construct the crowd in ways that produce various forms of subjectivity; second, how participants construct the crowd in ways that warrant social action. Extracts from the participants' transcripts are used to evidence the discursive repertoires that make these constructions possible, the subject positions and social practices warranted by them, as well as their implications for processes of governmentality, both at the level of the crowd – technologies of power, and at the level of the individual – technologies of self (Foucault, 1982). For coherence, this analysis is presented linearly; however, these two sections should not be considered as separate, but as interconnected sites of discursive practices.

3.1. Subjectification in the crowd

The participants' talk constructs various accounts of the crowd that problematise or normalise the crowd in general, or they problematise certain types of crowds but normalise others. All accounts are constructed as having implications to varying degrees, which are related to the crowd members' subjectivity: their embodied experience; rationality; senses of safety and danger; and risk taking. In constructing the crowd and the various subject positions within it, this analysis highlights the ways in which the crowd members are subject to the processes of governmentality, producing accounts of themselves as either compatible or problematic compared to the autonomous, neo-liberal ideal.

3.1.1. The crowd and rationality

The first three extracts construct the crowd in relation to rationality. Both Extract 1 and Extract 2 construct the crowd as irrational. However, whereas Extract 1 constructs both the crowd and the subject as irrational, Extract 2 constructs the subject as a rational agent within an irrational crowd. Extract 3 constructs both the crowd and the subject as rational.

Extract 1

R: How did you feel while you were in the crowd?

P4: I personally felt emotional. I was unable to identify why I was feeling emotional (.) My rational mind was speaking in the background, 'why are you feeling so <u>emotional</u>?' Yes I think it is natural that when you are inside a crowd and everybody is saying the same thing or shouting at the same time or singing the national anthem all at once. This triggers an emotional response. For me, it made me feel tearful. Not in a sad way but it makes you feel emotional. There is not necessarily a focus to it. You are not necessarily thinking of something but you get carried away in this moment of hyper nationalism or anger. But I feel it is separate from the actual cause of it. I think that your mind is not thinking about it. I still have this conversation with my rational side but not sure if that what everybody does (.) I am not saying that being emotional is not rational but I feel it is not <u>rational</u> when I do not know where these emotions come from.

In this extract, the participant constructs the feelings she experienced in the crowd as "emotional". This emotional response was "naturally" triggered by actions in the crowd such as "saying the same thing", "shouting at the same time" or "singing the national anthem all at once". These emotions had "no focus" and were "separate from the actual cause". The people in the crowd who experienced these emotions were "not necessarily thinking" of something but "carried away" in this moment of "hyper nationalism" or "anger". While in this state, she still had "a conversation" between herself and her "rational side" that questioned why she was so emotional. Despite the consciousness of the irrationality of her emotions, she lacked the capacity to understand or regulate them.

The participant differentiates between two emotional states: a "normal", rational state in which she knows from where her emotions come and an abnormal, "irrational" state that she experienced in the crowd. This account is reminiscent of Freud's (1900) personality theory that views personality as having rational and irrational as well as conscious and unconscious aspects. According to Freud, the continuous conflict between these aspects shapes a person's behaviour and emotion. Freud argued that people in a crowd enter a hypnotic state in which the irrational and unconscious aspects of their personalities dominate their behaviour; hence, they lose their capacity for self-regulation and become carried away in an intense and hyper-emotional state (Graumann & Moscovici, 1996). This account problematises crowd activities by constructing them as the product of irrational and unconscious processes. This construct has implications for the participant's subjectivity because she came to understand herself within the crowd as problematic compared to the ideal autonomous and rational individual who has the capacity for self-regulation (McNay,

2009). This account warrants no social action but avoiding
participation in crowd events or eliminating the crowd itself.

Extract 2

م١:انا كنت بحس الناس بتفقد نفسها ينجرفوا مع ناس ماشية(.) يعني لما الناس كانت
بتفكر يقتحموا وزارة الداخلية. في ناس كانت بتنجرف مع ده و ما كنوش <u>واعيين</u> ايه
خطورة ده. او ايه اللي ممكن يحصلهم او ده فعل صح او لا. او هل ده اللي احنا
عايزيين نعمله دلوقتي ولا لا. هل هيبعدنا عند هدفنا الاساسي ولا لا(.) ده انا كنت
بحسه. لكن انا شخصيا ما كنتش منجرفة(.) انا بقعد بتأني بشوف انا عايزةاعمل ايه .
و مقتنعة باللي بيحصل ولا مش مقتنعة. بروح مع الكرود لو انا مقتنعة باللي بيحصل
بس مش هجري و انا مش عارفة دول رايحيين فين او هيعملوا ايه ."

P1: I felt that people lost themselves and were carried away with
other people (.) When people were thinking about breaking into
the interior ministry, there were people who were carried away
with that. They were not <u>conscious</u> of the danger that it
presented, what could happen to them, whether that was right or
wrong, whether that was what we wanted to do, whether that
would take us away from our primary goal (.) That is what I felt.
But I myself was not carried away (.) I take my time to see what
I want to do and to think if I am convinced of what is happening
or not. I go with the crowd if I am convinced of what is
happening but I do not run if I do not know to where they are
going or what they are about to do.

In line with Extract 1, the second extract constructs crowd members as non-autonomous and irrational subjects who were "carried away". The participant gives an example by describing those people who were "carried away" with the idea of breaking into the interior ministry. They went along with this idea without being "conscious" of its "danger" or its morality (i.e., whether it was "right or wrong"). They were also unconscious of their own will; they did not know whether this action was what they "wanted" or whether it would serve their "primary goal".

This account is reminiscent of Le Bon's (1947) theory of the crowd, which proposes that crowd members can easily drift into hypnotic states in which they become suggestible and behave in irrational, destructive and immoral ways. Despite this negative account, the participant positions herself within the crowd as a rational subject with free-will who was not "carried away" and who independently based her decisions on what she "wanted" to do and what she thought was rational. She only went "along with the crowd" when she was "convinced" of their action and knew what they were doing. This subject position enables the participant to negotiate the negative account of the crowd in a way that warrants her participation in crowd action because she is capable of acting in a rational way within an irrational crowd. This subject position also warrants her taking actions that do not conform to those of the crowd when she is not convinced of them. At the same time, this position subjects the participant to "technologies of self" whereby she regulates her conduct within the crowd in line with the neoliberal ideal of the autonomous, responsible and self-governed individual.

Extract 3

م٤: لا ماكوناش منومين مغناطيسين. كنا خايفين و كنا متغاظين. انا في التمنتاشر يوم دول جالي امراض فهمت يعني ايه واحد ضغطة علي. ما كوناش في حالة ايفوريا(.) في التحرير طول الوقت كنت بترفلكت على حاجات كتيرة قوي. الناس كانت بدأت تتكلم في الدستور، فمقدرش افترض ان الناس دي كانت بتفكر بطريقة راشنل. الناس كانت بتفكر مثلا ايه اللي هيحصل لو مبارك اتنحي و جة بعده فتحي سرور ما هو اسوء منه. كل قرار كان بتراجع ميت مرة. و خصوصا ان كل واحد في الميدان عنده تلاتة اربعة من اهله مش موافقين انه ينزل الميدان. فانت محتاج تفكر في قرارتك على الاقل علشان تقنع الناس اللي مش في الميدان(.) احنا كنا مينوريتي و سط اغلبية رافضة اللي انت بتعمله. ده تحدي.

P4: No, We were not hypnotised. We were <u>afraid</u>. We were <u>angry</u>. In these eighteen days, I have got <u>illnesses</u>. I understood what it means to have high blood pressure. We were not in an euphoric state (.) The crowd in Tahrir Square were reflecting on many things all the time. They were talking about the constitution. I cannot assume that these people were thinking irrationally. For example, they were thinking about what would happen if Mubarak (*the Egyptian president at that time*) stepped down and Sorour (*the Egyptian parliament speaker at that time*) replaced him. He is even <u>worse.</u> Each decision was reviewed <u>hundred of</u> times. Especially everybody in the square had three or four of his or her family opposing the participation in the sit-in. We needed to think about our decisions at least to convince those who were not in the square (.) We were a minority in the middle of a majority that opposed what we were doing. That was a challenge.

In this extract, the participant constructs crowd members as rational thinkers. They were not in a state of relaxed suggestibility or "hypnotised" but "afraid" and "angry". In this context, the participant's subjectivity in the crowd is constructed as "embodied experience" (Foucault, 1994). Specifically, her emotions of anger and fear were linked to her body and manifested in the physical symptoms of "high blood pressure" illnesses. Crowd members did not experience an exaggerated and groundless "euphoric state"; rather, they were conscious agents engaging in continuous thinking processes (i.e., "reflecting on many things all the time"). They were thinking about complex issues such as "the constitution"; therefore, they could not be thinking "irrationally". They were examining what-if scenarios (e.g., "what would happen if Mubarak stepped down") as well as comparing and evaluating the alternatives. They concluded that Sorour, the parliament speaker who would be constitutionally appointed should Mubarak vacate his office, would be "even worse". Their decisions were made after being "reviewed hundreds of times". Because crowd members were a "minority" that faced a "majority" of citizens who were "not in the square" and who "opposed" the protesters' actions, crowd members "needed" to "think" to conclude decision that would be most likely to "convince" the majority.

This account is reminiscent of minority influence theories (Moscovici & Nemeth, 1974), which propose that a minority is capable of influencing the majority by producing views and actions that are consistent, flexible, and appealing as well as by presenting information that the majority does not know or expect. Thus, this construct resists the classic account of the hypnotised and euphoric crowd who experiences groundless states of exaggerated emotions that block rational thought (Le Bon, 1947). On the contrary, this construct normalises the crowd by construing its members as compatible with the neoliberal ideal of the autonomous and rational individual. However, this account subjects the participant to "technologies of self" that oblige her to regulate her conduct within the crowd in line with the neo-liberal values of rationality and responsibility.

3.1.2. The crowd and experience

In the following extract, the participant constructs her experience in a specific type of crowd in which the boundaries of personal space are pushed as stressful and irritating, whereas another type of crowd that has a common purpose is constructed as providing a sense of belonging and inclusion.

Extract 4

R: What was your idea on crowds before the 25th January? How did you feel about crowds and crowd events in general?

P4: I do not like being in crowded places (2) It is <u>stressful</u> and <u>irritating</u>. I think the dynamic can get selfish when people push, when people are not as aware of their surroundings. I probably have wider boundaries of personal space more than other people (.) There is a difference between a crowd in a shopping street and a crowd of people who are demonstrating about one thing or a crowd in a concert where everybody like this artist and enjoy the music. Then there is a different dynamic to this kind of crowd. I think it gives you a sense of belonging I suppose (.) If you go to a crowded area where people are there for the same reason, it blocks out other things and this one thing makes you feel included. But in other situations, being in a crowd can make you feel <u>isolated</u> even if you were around a lot of people.

In this extract, the participant describes herself as having wider "boundaries of personal space". This "personal space" is constructed as something that she "has" and that contains "boundaries" which assert ownership of a territory and separating it from the territory of others. This construction of personal space as private property is compatible with the neoliberal construction of the "self as an enterprise" and of "the autonomous individual" (McNay, 2009). The psychological concept of personal space in which the body is the centre might be seen as a "technology of the self" that serves not only to emphasise individual autonomy but also "discipline the body" in a way through which individuals come to regulate their physical contact with others (Foucault, 1988). The participant constructs crowds as "stressful" and "irritating" places in which the interpersonal dynamic can become "selfish" because people begin to "push" the boundaries of others' personal spaces and become less "aware" of their "surroundings". This account of the crowd is reminiscent of the psychological theories of personal space (Middlemist, Knowles & Matter, 1976), which might be seen as problematising the crowd because it is (by definition) a threat to the personal spaces of its members and therefore has negative emotional and psychological effects on them.

However, the participant resists this negative account by differentiating between two types of crowds that have different dynamics. In contrast to the "selfish" dynamic constructed earlier, a crowd in which people come together for a shared purpose is inclusive and provides a "sense of belonging".

In this extract, the participant constructs her subjectivity within one type of crowd as a negative "embodied experience" (Foucault, 1994) that connected the threat the crowd posed to her body to her thoughts and emotions. However, she also constructs her subjectivity in another type of crowd as a positive experience of inclusion enabled by the crowd's common purpose. This construct warrants her participation in crowd activities but only when the collective purpose of the crowd serves her interest.

3.1.3. The crowd and the senses of safety and danger

The next two extracts construct the crowd in relation to the participant's senses of safety and danger. Whereas Extract 5 constructs the crowd as a definite risk to the individual's autonomy, rationality and personal safety, Extract 6 constructs the crowd as a safe haven that provides crowd members with protection from the threats posed by the regime's repressive powers.

Extract 5

R: Do you mean that you feel freer and anonymous in a crowd than restricted and monitored?

P4: I think if you speak out alone in the crowd (2) People were getting kicked out of the square all the time. If people went up to the stage and said something that people did not like and then they get ejected from the square. I think if you speak out alone in the crowd, it is <u>a very risky</u> behaviour. If you go along with the crowd, it could be <u>risky</u> too. If people are running and you go along with them without knowing why you are running, you might be running toward the danger (.) I was in a situation when I walked out of a demonstration and we heard gunshots from where we left. I could not see what was fired but I heard gunfire and my friends started running (.) But I did not want to run but I ran after them. You do not think about the politics of it or why you were there. There is <u>a big</u> difference between why you were there for in the first place and what you end up actually doing (.)You probably use different types of mental processes.

The participant constructs "speaking out alone" within a crowd as a "very risky behaviour" because individuals who said something that the crowd did not like were "ejected from the square". In this sense, the crowd is constructed as an oppressive entity that enforced conformity on its members and punished individuals who publicly expressed ideas of which "it" did not approve. Therefore, being within a crowd is a risk to the autonomy and free will of its members. On the other hand, "going along with" the crowd could also be "risky". In this context, the participant provides a personal example when she heard gunshots but was unable to see what was fired. The participant constructs herself as a non-autonomous subject who ran after her friends although she "did not want to run". The participant's actions are constructed as out of her control and not in accord with what she "wanted" or her free will. The mental processes that the participant "used" within the crowd were pathologised by constructing them as "different types of mental processes" that do not allow people to "think" about ramifications of actions or "why you were there". Using these abnormal mental processes, the participant behaved in a way that differed from what she was "there for in first place".

In this sense, the participant's subjectivity in the crowd is problematic in relation to the neoliberal ideal of the autonomous and self-regulated individual. This construct is reminiscent of Le Bon's (1947) negative account of the crowd, which proposes that crowd members lose their autonomy and behave in irrational, destructive and immoral ways that they would not do so as individuals. This account constructs the crowd as a definite and continuous threat to individuals' autonomy, rationality, capacity for self-regulation and personal safety. Therefore, it problematises the crowd and warrants avoiding crowd events.

Extract 6

م٥: بص هقولك حاجة(.) لما كنا بنلاقي حشد كنا بننزل في وسطه. كان فيه مجموعات كبيرة مش هينفع يتسيطر عليها بسهولة. ان كنت بحس بامان بصراحة(.) على ايام تسعة و عشرين تلاتين و معركة الجمل حصلت لما كنا بنمشي في مجموعات صغيرة كنت بحس وقتها بالأمان. لما كنت بنزل من بيتنا و بركب تاكسي كنت ببقى مرعوب. انت وحيد ونازل دي فكرة مرعبة في حد ذاتها لغاية ما تلاقي

مجموعة اصحاب ماشية سوا ولد و بنت و تلاقي في تسلسلات ماشية ورا بعضها (.) همه مش متسلسلين لكن تحس ان الناس متوجهة لهدف معين. في حتة معينة بفهم انه نزلني هنا. و بتحرك معاهم. المهم و انا بتحرك معاهم. الناس كانت ساعتها مبسوطة بالموضوع و احد قال لي وانا ماشي الله عليكم يا شباب مصر. لغاية ما توصل الميدان(.) و كان بيبقى فيه لجان التفتيش في الميدان. انا عادي كنت بستسلم لها مفيش مشاكل. ده بيتعمل علشانا و العيال دي مننا فينا.

P5: Listen; let me tell you something (.) Whenever we found a crowd, we went to its centre. There were big groups that were not easily controlled. Honestly, I felt safe (.) By the 29th and the 30th January when the Battle of the Camel happened, I felt safe when moving in small groups. On the occasions when I left home and took a taxi, I was terrified. I was alone. That was a terrifying idea in itself. Whenever I saw a group of friends walking together, a young man and young woman, lines of people following each other (.) Actually they were not in lines but they seemed to be going to a particular destination. I understood that is the point to get off and move with them. Anyway while moving with them, people were happy with what was happening. Somebody told me while walking 'God bless you the youth of Egypt.' Till you arrive to the square (.) There were security committees. I surrendered to them. No problem. That is done for us and these guys belong to us.

This account constructs the crowd as a safe haven in which the participant seeks protection from the threats of the regime. Whereas "big groups of people" are constructed as not easily "controlled", the participant constructs himself as vulnerable and terrified when alone. This fear is understandable in the context of the Battle of the Camel, when state-funded thugs, some of whom rode camels, attacked Tahrir Square and killed dozens of demonstrators on the fifth day of the sit-in. Therefore, the participant joined "the centre" of the crowd "whenever" he could find one and moved around "in small groups" to feel safe. This account constructs individuality as a state of vulnerability and privileges the collectivity of the crowd by constructing it as a means of metaphorical and physical resistance to oppression as well as a protection from the lethal power used by the regime. In contrast to the neoliberal ethical agenda that promotes the values of individuality and self-reliance, this account creates a space for a more social understanding of the self as empowered and emboldened by collective bonds of solidarity to others.

Once the participant arrived at Tahrir Square, he willingly "surrendered" to the security committees (i.e., the disciplinary gaze of the crowd) that were checking the identities of every person who entered the square. These practices of surveillance are rationalised and normalised by constructing them as being done "for us" by fellow crowd members (i.e., "belong to us"). Thus, whereas this construct warrants resisting the power of the state, it does not enable any room for resistance to the "technologies of power" internal to the crowd that operated through the security committees.

3.1.4. The crowd and risk taking

The following extract constructs the crowd as on the edge between fascism and freedom whereas the crowd member is constructed as a risk taker who negotiates his position in relation to the opportunities and the risks entailed in crowd activity.

Extract 7

م٥: يعني الحشد لينقلك للفاشية لينقلك للحرية. و ده رعب الليبرالية من فكرة الحشد . فكرة الليبرالية اللي طول عمرها حاطة نفسها في النص مابين الفاشية و الشيوعية. علشان كده الليبرالية طول الوقت عايزة ترعب الناس من فكرة الحشد. الحشد في حد ذاته على شفا حاجتين يا فعلا الفاشية يا الثورة الشعبية (.) وانا طول الوقت باخد الرسك. يعني البنت اللي نازلة من البيت ، على فكرة هيه بتاخد الرسك. بس هي بتاخد رسك أعلى. فتخيل الستات اللي هي نازلة مش بس رسكينج حياتها هي لكن فكرة جسدها كمان(.) بس ده رسك لازم تاخده(.) زي ما تكون بتلعب رشن روليت بفكرة الموت.

P5: The crowd carries you either to fascism or freedom. That is the reason why liberalism that always locates itself in the middle between fascism and communism is scared of the idea of <u>the crowd</u>. That is the reason way Liberalism wants to make people scared of the crowd. Actually the crowd is on the edge of two things: either fascism or a popular revolution (.) I take the risk every time. The young woman, who leaves her house to join the crowd, takes a risk, but a higher risk. These young women do not only risk their lives but their bodies as well (.) But that is a risk that we must take (.) like playing Russian roulette.

This extract constructs the crowd as "on the edge between fascism and freedom", entailing the possibility to "carry" people to either "fascism or popular revolution". Liberalism is constructed as "scared" of the "idea of the crowd" because it poses a threat to its form of government that locates itself between "fascism and communism". Liberalism attempts to solve the crowd problem by "making people scared of the crowd". However, the participant, who is aware of the opportunities and the risks that the crowd entails, constructs himself as a "risk taker… every time" that he joins the crowd. A young woman who willingly leaves the safety of "her home" to join the crowd takes a greater risk because she not only places her "life" at risk but also puts "her body" at the risk of sexual harassment from the crowd. The significance of the risk of sexual harassment can be understood in light of the values of Egyptian society that emphasise the purity of a women's body as central to the notion of honour. In this context, the risk entailed in joining the crowd is constructed as taken willingly and consciously, like playing "Russian Roulette".

Although this account problematises the crowd by constructing it as a potential risk for fascism, it also constructs it as an opportunity for freedom and a popular revolution. The implication of this multifaceted account can be seen in the participant's position as a risk taker. This subject position is compatible with the neoliberal conceptualisation of the individual as a prudent risk-taker and entrepreneur who continuously sifts through available options to maximise benefits and minimise harms (Marques, 2010). In this sense, this account normalises the crowd by constructing it in terms of a network of enterprise that entails the possibilities of gain and loss, which the crowd member manages as a rational risk taker to maximise his freedom.

3.2. The crowd as warranting social action

This section examines the participants' constructions of the crowd in relation to social action. These constructions are presented within three categories: First, how the participants construct the ways whereby the crowd regulated its members' conduct; second, how they construct the ways whereby the crowd regulated the participation of women; and third, how they construct the ways whereby the crowd regulated violence. All these accounts have different implications for social practices and highlight different strategies of resistance to the self-regulating processes of the crowd.

3.2.1. The crowd and self-regulation

The next two extracts construct the crowd in Tahrir square in relation to the self-regulatory processes of the crowd. The first extract constructs the crowd as developing a set of norms through which its members regulated their conduct. The second extract constructs the crowd as being regulated by various committees that were specialised for certain tasks.

Extract 8

م١: تطور النورمز بتاعت الحشد بيحصل كرد فعل لحاجات كانت بتحصل في
لحظتها(.) مثلا شخص بيمسك طوبة و هيرميها علي ظابط و فجأة الناس بتطور
نورم و بتقول انها هتبقى سلمية. خلاص كلنا هنعمل مع بعض انها هتبقى <u>سلمية</u>.
فكلنا هنحاول نوقف الشخص ده. كان فيه ناس بتهتف هتافات إسلامية. الناس كرد
فعل كانت بتحاول تسكتهم. فطرنا النورمز انها مش هتبقى ثورة إسلامية و هتبقى
سلمية. و هتبقى كذا و هتبقى كذا(.) لو حد حاول يضايق حد. كرد فعل الناس بتعمل
كدة و ناس بتنضم ليهم و بعدين ده بيبقى السلوك العام.

P2: Crowd norms were developing instantly as a reaction to things that were happening (.) For example, somebody picked a rock and was about to throw it at one police officer. Immediately people developed norms and started chanting 'peaceful protest'. That is it. Everybody worked together to keep it peaceful. All of us tried to stop this person. There were some people chanting 'Islamic revolution'. As a reaction to that, everybody was trying to silence them. We developed the norms that it would be non-Islamic revolution and it would be peaceful. And it would be this and that (.) If somebody harassed another person, people did something and other people joined them. And then that became a general conduct.

In this account, the participant constructs the crowd as "developing" norms in "a reaction" to "things that were happening". When one crowd member began to throw a rock at a police officer, people "immediately developed norms" which they declared by chanting "peaceful revolution". This crowd instantly acquired an identity as being peaceful. Thus, a collective action was taken by the crowd to regulate its members' behaviours so that they remained in line with this identity. Hence, crowd members "worked together" to keep the protest "peaceful" by restricting one of its member's behaviour: "all of us" tried to "stop" this person from throwing the rock. When "some people" attempted to declare a different identity by chanting "Islamic revolution", the crowd collectively acted to "silence them". These self-regulatory actions are legitimised by constructing them as serving the collectively developed norms and identity: "We developed the norms that it would be a non-Islamic revolution, and it would be peaceful". The crowd also developed these norms to protect their members "as a reaction" to an incident in which "somebody harassed another person". To stop this offensive behaviour, people "did something", and then they were "joined" by "other people". Later, this behaviour became "the general conduct". This account is reminiscent of Emergent Norm Theory (Turner & Killian, 1987), which proposes that there is no norm to govern crowd behaviour when it coalesces. Norms emerge through a process of social interaction in which people look to others for cues that indicate what to expect. As time goes by, these norms become entrenched, and there is pressure against non-conformity.

This account constructs crowd members in line with neoliberal values (McNay, 2009), as rational individuals who developed their own norms to meet the demands of reality and serve their collective interests (e.g., maintaining their collective identity and protecting members from harassment). Thus, this account rationalises the self-regulatory processes of the crowd and warrants actions in order to enforce conformity to crowd norms.

Extract 9

م١: ما هي كانت لجان شعبية(.) ما همه كانوا بيعملوا ايه ؟ كان بيبقي فيه لجان. كان متطوعين. الواحد ده بقى ممكن يكون إخوان او من بيجي واحد يقول احنا محتاجين شباب ستة ابريل ممكن يكون من أي حتة. فيقولوا احنا محتاجين متطوعين(.) فيبتدوا يكتبوا اسأميهم وأرقام تليفوناتهم و يوزعوا التاسكس. فالتاسك دي هننمن المداخل ازاي . تنضيف لو هنضف. ففيه مجموعات من الناس بتعمل كل حاجة. اللي بيعمل ده كلة ممكن الإخوان المسلمين حركة ستة ابريل. كنت بشوف ناس من كل الطوائف و التيارات السياسية. في الأخر بيعملوا ده تحت اسم <u>فولنتير</u>. فالمتطوع بيروح بغض النظر عن القيادة(.) مادام هوة في خدمة التحرير، و الهدف الاسمي لإسقاط النظام. انا لو حد من الإخوان قال لي تبقي متطوعة في حملة ايه . ماشي. مش هركز ان ده إخوان مسلمين. قد ما هركز اعمل حاجة تخدم الثورة.

P1: There were people committees (.) That was what they did. There were committees. People used to come and say we need volunteers (.) These people could be from the Muslim Brotherhood (*an Egyptian Islamist opposition movement*), the Youth of the 6th of April Movement (*an Egyptian secular opposition movement*) or from any other movement. And then they wrote down names, phone numbers and then allocated tasks: to secure the entrances, to clean. There were groups of people for all things. Those people were from the Muslim Brotherhood, 6th of April movement and people from all political streams. At the end, they worked under the title, <u>volunteers.</u> The volunteers joined regardless of the leadership (.) as long as they were serving the revolution and the overall goal of bringing the regime down.

In this extract, the participant constructs the Tahrir Square crowd as a well-organised entity that relied on what could be called, a bureaucracy. This bureaucracy is constructed as having "leadership", "volunteers" and "committees" that are responsible for various "tasks", including securing the entrances, cleaning and "all things". This bureaucracy has a database for its members' information including their names and phone numbers. Constructing the members of these committees as "volunteers" implies that their participation was not motivated by personal financial gain but by the collective "overall goal of bringing the regime down". These volunteers are also constructed as coming from diverse backgrounds: from the secular 6th April Movement, the Islamist Muslim Brotherhood and "all political streams" that came together despite their differences, to "serve the revolution". This positive account of the crowd as having a practical, specialised, well-structured, diverse and inclusive bureaucracy normalises the crowd and obliges the participant to take part in the action of its committees.

This construct also rationalises the practices of these committees, including the security committee that was responsible for securing the entrances of Tahrir Square and checking the identity of every person who entered the square. This committee, which is constructed in several accounts in the transcript, including Extract 7, could be seen as an internal surveillance system that operated through individualisation techniques that rendered crowd members as constantly visible to the crowd's disciplinary gaze (Foucault, 1977). These individualisation techniques operated also at the level of the committee by assigning specific tasks to each member and recording their names and phone numbers. Thus, this account not only normalises the crow but also legitimises its self-regulatory practices. By constructing these self-regulatory practices as positive and productive and as aiming to serve the overall goal of the revolution, this account leaves no room to resist these practices.

The preceding two extracts construct the self-regulatory processes of the crowd, which operated through an internalised set of norms and a bureaucratic network of committees. The following two sections explore the implications of these processes with regard to the women in the crowd and the crowd's use of violence.

3.2.2.   The crowd and gender

The following two extracts construct crowd action with regard to women. Whereas Extract 10 constructs the crowd as developing norms

that empower women to challenge the social norms of society,
Extract 11 constructs the crowd as manipulating the position of its
female members to achieve certain goals through two techniques:
empowerment and sexual harassment.

Extract 10

م٣: البوندريز بين العام و الشخصي. يعني احنا كنا بنبقى نايميين على الأرض
ستات و ده مش مقبول في مجتمعنا. الأكل موضوع خاص و بقينا نأكل في الشارع.
الشارع ده ما كنش بتاعنا و بالذات وسط البلد(٣) حصل دياندفيدوليزيشن لان الناس
اكويرد هوية مجموعة و علشان كدة بيتبقى مور بورفول. بتيبقى اقل خوفا و أكثر
شجاعة(.) ده بان لي جدا في يوم المسيرة النسائية انا كنت مكتئبة جدا و بسبب بابايا
و بسبب اني لما سافرت و رجعت شوفت الكوفينز فكنت منهارة. فلما رحت المسيرة
و كنت مكتئبة قوي فجأة حسيت نفسي مور باورفل ، لان الكرود مور باورفل من
اني أبقى لوحدي. اتز سيربريوتك ، لمل كنت واقفة في وسط عدد كبير من الستات
بتهتف لحقهم حسيت لأول مرة بأحاسيس اني مرتاحة اني انا ست و فخورة اني انا
ست. و مش قرفانة من الستات المصريين. يو جت انبورد باي زا جروب .

P3: The boundaries between the private and the public were
removed. Women were sleeping on the ground which is not
accepted in our society. Eating is a private thing but we were
eating on the streets. The streets were not ours in the past,
especially the downtown ones (3) People were de-individualised
because they acquired a group identity and therefore they
became more <u>powerful</u>, less afraid and braver. That became
obvious to me during the Women's March. I was depressed

because of my father's death and because I saw his coffin
when I went back. Therefore I was devastated. And when I went
to the march while I was depressed, I felt suddenly more
powerful. Because being in a crowd is more powerful than being
on my own. It is therapeutic. When I was standing in the middle
a big number of women chanting for their rights, I felt for the
first time comfortable with being a woman and proud of being a
woman and not despising Egyptian women. You get empowered
by the group.

In this extract, the participant constructs the crowd as a source of
empowerment for its members in general and women in particular. This
empowerment is demonstrated in the way that the crowd developed new
norms to enable its female members to challenge social norms and
remove the "boundaries" between the "private" and the "public".
Although existing within a patriarchal society that restricts women's
public activity, the crowd enabled women to act in ways that were not
socially "accepted" (e.g., "sleeping on the ground" and "eating in
public") and claim ownership of "the streets", which are constructed as
"not ours". Contrary to classic accounts of deindividuation (i.e., the
process through which individuals lose their sense of self, rationality
and morality in a crowd ; Diener 1979; Festinger, Pepitone &
Newcomb, 1952; Singer, Brush & Lublin, 1965), this participant
constructs a positive account of deindividuation as the process through
which individuals in the crowd acquired "a group identity". This

identity was empowering, reassuring, and made the participant "more powerful", "braver" and "less afraid" than when she was "on her own". The participant who was "depressed" and "devastated" because of her father's death constructs her experience of being in the "middle of a big number" of women who the crowd enabled to "chant for their rights" as "therapeutic". This experience was therapeutic because it enabled her to accept herself for the "first time" as a woman (i.e., to be "comfortable with" and "proud of" being a woman).

The construct of the crowd as a remover of the boundaries between the "public" and the "private" is reminiscent of post-structuralist ideas regarding the Public Sphere. Hardt and Negri (2009), drawing on Foucault's ideas, argued that the distinction between the public and private spheres is founded on the neoliberal account of property that presupposes a clear-cut separation between interests of individuals. In this sense, this construct of the crowd creates a space for an alternative understanding of the self as situated in a single boundary-less sphere with others. By constructing the deindividuation process as making a crowd member more powerful and braver than the individual on his or her own, this construct privileges the state of the de-individualised self. This creates a space for a more social understanding of the self as emboldened and empowered by collective bonds of solidarity to others, compared with the neoliberal ideal of the autonomous individual.

Thus, this account privileges the crowd by constructing it positively as empowering and therapeutic, particularly to women. It also warrants crowd members acting in ways that challenge social norms as well as the boundaries between private and public spheres.

Extract 11

م٣: فيه كلام كتير بس انا مش متعمقة فيه(.) ان التحرش الجنسي اداة للتحكم في الستات في الاماكن العامة. ندخلهم ما ندخلهمش ده بمزاجنا و هنستخدم الوسيلة دي علشان نمشيهم. دي البوليتكس بتاعت التحرش الجنسي. في الحشد فكان فيه قرار جمعي ان احنا محتاجين الستات ما يخافوش محتاجين الستات ينزلوا. محتاجين الستات يقفوا في أول المظاهرة. و يقودوا المظاهرة و نردد و راهم (.) و بعدين فيه احساس اننا مش محتاجين الستات. الحشد قرر اننا هنسيبهم في حالهم دلوقتي. و بعد كدة لازم يرجعوا ولازم يقلوا.

P3: There is a lot on that but I only have limited knowledge (.) Sexual harassment is a tool to control women in public places. To let women in or not, it is up to them. They will use this tool to make women leave. That is the politics of sexual harassment. Within the crowd, there was a collective decision that women were needed. Women should not feel threatened because the crowd needed them to join. They needed women to stand in the front of the demonstration, to lead the demonstration and they would repeat after them (.) Later, there was the feeling that they did not need women anymore. They decided not to bother women at that time. But later women should leave.

This participant constructed the crowd as manipulative in the context of an incident of sexual harassment that occurred during the Tahrir Square demonstrations following Mubarak's resignation. In the first eighteen days, the crowd made a "collective decision" to allow women to participate in the sit-in because they were "needed". In contrast to the Egyptian societal norms that restrain women's activities in public, the crowd developed new norms that enabled women "to join" crowd events, "stand in the front" and "lead the demonstration". The crowd not only empowered women to lead the demonstrations but also legitimised and asserted their leadership by "repeating after them".

By enabling women to stand at the front of the demonstration, the crowd used women to protect the rest of the demonstrators from police violence and promote a positive image of the crowd as inclusive, liberal and peaceful. However, once the sit-in achieved its primary goal of forcing Mubarak from power, the crowd felt that they did not "need" women any more. Therefore, they used "sexual harassment... to control" women in "public places" to make them "leave". In this account, the crowd is not essentially empowering (as in Extract 10) or oppressive (as in Extract 5); rather, a rational and dynamic group of men that made conscious and pragmatic decisions and developed norms to manipulate women to meet their needs. This account is reminiscent of a feminist account of sexual harassment as a method of control that operates on the body of women and seeks to internalise in them a feeling of threat in order to regulate their social action in public places (Smart & Smart, 1978). In this sense, sexual harassment and empowerment could be seen as technologies of power internal to the crowd by which the female crowd members' conduct is regulated through a dynamic and changing set of norms.

Thus, although this account constructs the crowd in negative terms as manipulative and selectively oppressive towards women, it also normalises the crowd by constructing it in line with the neoliberal values as a rational group that manages its resources to fulfil its collective needs (McNay, 2009). However, by gendering the crowd and constructing it as a manipulative and oppressive group of men, this account problematises the norms and the self-regulatory practices of the crowd.

3.2.3. The crowd and violence

The following two extracts construct two ways through which violent behaviour was regulated within the crowd. Extract 12 constructs the destructive behaviour within the crowd as regulated at the level of individual crowd members through the voice of rationality. Extract 13 constructs the crowd's violence as regulated at the level of the crowd through collective decision-making processes.

Extract 12

م٥: انا ما بنكرهاش انه طول الوقت في اللحظة دي ممكن تكون قوة تدميرية. المنطق و السلوك الحضاري اللي كان بيتقال علي الحشد كان بيبقى صوت السلطة

على فكرة. صوت السلطة هو الحفاظ علي الذات و سلف ريزفيشن بطريقة معينة(.) هديلك مثل انا و صديقتي كنا قدام ماسبيرو في نفس اليوم اللي بيتخلع الصبح ، انا بطبيعتي مماين. لما صديقتي ابتدت تتحرك انا أتحركت معاها. انا كنت بتكلم اني عايز اجيب سهير شلبي من شعرها. انا كنت بهرج طبعا. و فيه واحد واقف بماشين جن من الجيش. المهم احنا عايزين ندخل نحرق التلفزيون و صوت المنطق و العقل بتاع الناس يقولك لا التلفزيون ده بتاعنا. حرام المعدات حرام المشعارف ايه. المعدات دي لينا احنا، النظام زايل لكن احنا اللي قعدين. و قعدنا نقول هل الثورة بتاعتنا دي ثورة محافظة و لا مش ثورة محافظة. و فكرة ان الإنجليز أعجبوا بيك جدا. و فكرة ان الإنجليز أعجبوا بيك جدا جدا بفكرة ان المصريين يقوموا بثورة و ينضفوا آثارها بعديها. ان دي أفكار محافظة أكيد الإنجليز يموتوا فيها(.) الناس فاقت منها انهه احنا كنا محتاجين لحظة كان فيها جوانب تدميرية. انه انت لوعايز تهد دولة او تهد نظام كان لابد منها. و اللي جاب حال البلد انك حرقت <u>ستميت قسم</u> في سبع ساعات.

P5: I do not deny that the crowd can be a destructive force at any moment. The rationality and the civility that the crowd was known for were the voice of authority. The voice of authority is self-preserving in some ways (.) For example, I and my friend were at the national TV building on the same day Mubarak was removed. When my friend started to move I moved with her. I was saying that I wanted to drag Soher Shalby (*the head of the Egyptian state-owned television network*) by her hair. I was not going to do that. There was a soldier with a machine gun there. Anyway we wanted to break into the TV building and set it on fire. The voice of rationality was saying that the national TV belonged to us, it was waste to burn the equipment, and this equipment was ours. The regime will leave but we will not. We were wondering if our revolution was conservative or not. The English admired the fact that the Egyptian had a revolution and then cleaned after it. These are conservative ideas that the English are fond of (.) We released later that we needed a moment with destructive sides. If you want to destroy a state or a regime, you need this moment. What changed the country was that we set 600 police stations on fire in seven hours.

This account constructs the crowd in Tahrir Square as a potentially "destructive force", but at the same time, one that is known for its "civility" and "rationality" which are the "voices of authority". Unsurprisingly, this participant (who is a social science Ph.D. student at a Western university) constructs the crowd in a way reminiscent of Foucault's concept of governmentality. According to Foucault, power operates not only through repression but also through techniques of social control that normalise and privilege certain ways of being, values and behaviour. These techniques operate through discourses such as "civility" and "rationality" that get internalised by the individual crowd members and guide their conduct in ways that restrain the destructive force entailed in the crowd and hence preserve the status quo. In this context, although the crowd wanted "to break into" the state TV building that was the regime's propaganda machine and "set it on fire", the internalised "voice of rationality" was constructed as restraining crowd members from this violent behaviour. This restraint was because the "equipment… belongs to us" and not "the regime"; therefore, it was "waste" to burn them. This argument is in line with the neoliberal ideal of the rational individual who is capable of self-management to maximise gain and minimise risk .

The participant constructs this voice of rationality in positive terms as self-preserving. For example, it is constructed as restraining him from attempting to attack Soher Shalby, the head of the national television, because trying to enter the TV building to attack her might have placed him at risk of being shot by the "solider with the machine gun" who guarded the building. However, these civilised behaviours, such as "cleaning" at the end of the sit-in, were constructed in negative terms as "conservative". Cleaning the square removed the evidence of the violence committed by the police and demonstrators, such as burned cars, rocks, bloodstains and bullets. Thus, the square returned to its previous state, thereby removing the signifier of change. By constructing rationality and civility as self-preserving, on one hand, and "conservative" and the "voices of authority", on the other, this account allows room for resistance against the "technologies of self" that operate through discourses of "civility" and "rationality" upon which crowd members regulate their conduct and restrain themselves from the destructive behaviour "needed" to change the regime. Furthermore, by constructing the act of burning 600 police stations in a few hours as "what changed the country", this account warrants acting in destructive and violent ways when violence serves the crowd's radical goals (e.g., "to destroy a state or a regime").

Extract 13

فالقرار الجمعي ما كنش في بس في مظاهرات سلمية لا و في المظاهرة اللي كان فيها عنف كل الناس كانت مجمعة على انه ممكن تحدف طوب و كل الناس كانت مجمعة انه محدش يحدف قزاز(.) الفرن فاتح و صاحبة قاعد قدامه و الطوب بيتحدف جنبهم و كل الناس مجمعة ان الطوب مش هيتحدف كدة. و إننا مش هنخش نسرق محل و الهدف بتاع العنف <u>واضح قوي</u>(.) القرار الجمعي مش بس كان في الحشد بتاع ميدان التحرير ده كان <u>في كل حتة</u>. لان القصص الي انت بتسمعها من مصر هيه هيه بشكل <u>مرعب</u> فعلا ازاي القرار كان بتخذ انا مش عارفة ، كل الكلام عن انه فيه نواه تنظيمية كلام فارغ. كان فيه وعي جمعي انا مش فاهماه بيترجر أول ما بيحصل ثريت. و بيعمل نفس الحاجة لاننا اصلا عايشيين علي انفورمال نيت وركس. طول عمرنا و ان اصلا الدولة مش موجودة(.) فيه ديسيشن مايكينج بروسيس بنعملها يوميا. فظهرت اكتر لان الثريت كان اعلى(.) التينشن كان بيحصل في اللجان الشعبية انه فيه تلاتة عايزيين يفتشوا كل واحد معدي و فيه تلاتة لا. فيه ناس كانت عايزة تحرق و فيه ناس مش عايزة تحرق. كانت فيه تنشن طول الوقت لكن القرار الجمعي كان اننميس طول الوقت(.) مش عارفة (.) الهرد منتالتي ؟ لا انت مش بتسمع كلام حد انت بتشارك في القرار. انت مش بتحس انك منقاد للقرار انت واعي للقرار. يعني انا ما حدفتش طوب بس انا فاهمة و متعاطفة.

P3: The collective decision was not only present in peaceful demonstrations but also in violent demonstrations. People were in agreement that it was allowed to throw rocks and all people

were in agreement not to throw glass (.) The bakery was open
and its owners were sitting in front of it. The rocks were thrown
close to them but all people were in agreement not to throw
rocks at their direction and not to loot the shop. The target of the
violence was clear (.) The collective decision was not only
present in the crowd in Tahrir Square but everywhere. The
stories you hear in Egypt were similar in a scary way. How was
the decision taken? I do not know. The suggestion that this was
due to an organised core is nonsense. There was a collective
awareness which I do not understand, that gets triggered by a
threat. Is that because we live on informal networks? All the
time, the state does not exist (.) There is a collective decision
making process we engage with on a daily basis and it appeared
clearer because the threat was higher (.) There was tension in
local committees, there were members who wanted to search
everybody passing by and there were those who did not. Some
people wanted to commit arson and some people did not. There
was tension all the time and the decisions were unanimous all
the time (.) I do not know (.) Is that a herd mentality? No, you
do not conform to somebody else's decision. You take part in
taking the decision. You are not submissive to the decision but
you are aware of it. I did not throw rocks but I understand and
sympathise with this action.

In this extract, the participant constructs crowd members as collective and autonomous decision makers in "peaceful" and "violent" demonstrations. In the violent demonstrations, the crowd members "were in agreement" on what forms of violence were "allowed" (i.e., "to throw rocks" but "not… glass"). Because the demands of the protest in Tahrir Square were summed up in the slogan "bread, freedom and dignity", crowd members agreed not to direct their violence at the bakery that produced bread but at the oppressive police force that violated their freedom and dignity. The crowd is also constructed as a moral group who collectively agreed "not to loot the shop". In contrast to the classic account of crowd action as irrational, immoral and destructive (Le Bon, 1947), this account normalises crowd's violent actions by constructing them as moral, rational and target-focused.

The "collective decision making" was not exclusive to Tahrir Square but was "everywhere". The similarities of the stories that this participant heard from across Egypt were "scary" to her because she "did not know" how these collective decision-making processes worked. These processes were not due to political organisations; rather, they seemed to be working according to a mechanistic, natural process as whereby the "collective awareness" was "triggered by a threat". This collective awareness is constructed as being based on an "informal support network" that people "live on" to fulfil their needs because the "state" that "does not exist" obviously cannot provide for its citizens. This awareness did not cause all crowd members to think or behave in the same way. Some members of the local committees "wanted" to search every passer-by or commit arson, whereas other members did "not want" to take these actions. This conflict of wills caused "continuous tension". This construct negates the classic account of the crowd as having a "herd mentality" (Le Bon, 1947) in which people conform to the collective norms. Thus, the crowd members are constructed in line with the neoliberal ideal as autonomous and conscious decision makers who do "not conform" to "somebody else's decision"; rather, they "take part" in the decision-making process that aims to fulfil their needs and avoid risks. In this context, the participant constructs herself as an autonomous individual who was able "to understand" and "sympathise with" the crowd's action while they were throwing rocks but "did not throw rocks" herself. This subject position warrants individual crowd members taking actions independently within the crowd.

This account constructs the crowd's behaviour in general and its violent behaviour in particular as regulated through the collective decision-making processes of autonomous crowd members in order to fulfil their needs and avoid risks. This construct normalises these self-regulatory processes and warrants crowd members acting in violent ways towards legitimate targets such as the oppressive police.

4.   Conclusion and critique

This section revisits and discusses the research aims and questions in light of the analysis. Based on this, recommendations for crowd activists are presented. This research is also evaluated, and implications for future research are explored.

4.1.   Revisiting the research aims, key analytic foci and recommendations

This research aimed to explore how those who participated in the Tahrir Square sit-in during the Egyptian Revolution constructed the crowd with regard to this experience. This aim was warranted by the lack of discursive research on crowds from the perspective of their members and reflected in the research questions:

How do the Egyptian demonstrators who participated in the Tahrir Square sit-in construct the crowd with regard to this experience?

How do these constructions serve to normalise, problematise or privilege the crowd?

What subject positions are enabled by these constructions, and what are the implications for action of these subject positions, particularly with regard to crowd action?

How are crowd members subject to the practices of governmentality at the level of the crowd (disciplinary power) and the level of the individual (self-regulation)?

These research questions were answered through the presentation of two main categories. The first category outlined some of the ways in which crowd members construed the crowd in relation to subjectification: rationality, experience, the senses of safety and danger, and risk taking. These were constructed in relation to material and discursive accounts of the crowd as either compatible or problematic compared to   the neoliberal values of autonomy and rationality. The crowd members reproduced a wider societal account of the crowd as problematic that poses risks to individual rationality, autonomy, personal space and safety. At the same time, however, the crowd members resisted this negative account by producing an alternative account of the crowd as rational, and providing a sense of inclusion and protection from state oppression. Most accounts were complex and multifaceted and constructed the crowd as entailing both risks and opportunities. These accounts warranted various subject positions for the crowd members which enabled them to negotiate the problematic account of the crowd. For example, Extract 2 constructed the participant as a rational and autonomous individual even though she was within an irrational crowd. Moreover, Extract 7 constructed the participant as a risk taker in a crowd on the edge between fascism and freedom. A variety of strategies for resisting the negative account of the crowd were explored. However, these attempts at resistance still reinforced the neoliberal ideal of the autonomous individual.

The second category of constructs outlined some of the ways in which the crowd was constructed in relation to social action. The first two extracts constructed the crowd as self-regulated by two methods of social control: a set of collective norms that guided the crowd members' conduct in line with their identity and a bureaucratic network of committees that served as an internal system of surveillance. These self-regulatory processes of the crowd were normalised by constructing them as rational, productive and aiming to minimise risk and achieve the crowd's goals. By normalising these processes, oppressive actions towards crowd members were warranted to enforce conformity to crowd norms. Although these constructs enabled resistance against negative accounts of the crowd, they subjected crowd members to "technologies of self" and "technologies of power" internal to the crowd by obliging them to conform to and participate in enforcing conformity to crowd self-regulatory processes.

In constructing the crowd in relation to women and violence, the crowd members produced complex and multifaceted accounts of the crowd. On one hand, the crowd was constructed as empowering women to challenge social norms and the boundaries between the private and the public spheres. In addition, crowd violence was constructed positively as self-regulated in a rational, moral and productive manner. These constructs served to create a space for a more social understanding of the self compared to the neo-liberal ideal of the autonomous individual and to normalise crowd violence. On the other hand, the crowd was constructed as manipulating women and controlling their participation in crowd activity by means of sexual harassment and empowerment. In addition, crowd rationality and civility were constructed negatively as "the voices of authority" that seek to preserve the status quo by preventing the violence needed to achieve radical political change. These constructs warranted that crowd members challenging the crowd norms and self-regulatory processes as well as resisting the discourses of rationality and civility.

Based on this analysis, I tentatively put forward some recommendations for activists who are inspired to challenge political oppression and social inequality by means of crowd action. The first is to suggest we look at the way in which crowds are constructed as the site of power struggles between the status quo and political change. Social control operates through negative accounts of the crowd that delegitimise crowd action and legitimise the suppressive practices that the state uses to eliminate the crowd. The discursive practices permitted by these negative accounts have a real effect not only on the public support for crowd action but also on the subjectivity of crowd members themselves. Resistance to these discursive practices allows room for alternative accounts and subjectivities to be constructed. Therefore, practices that construct positive accounts of crowd action are recommended. For example, it might be helpful for members of sit-ins to communicate with the media and the local community to publicise their aims and values in ways that challenge the negative account of the crowd and highlight the major role of crowd action in resisting social injustice and political oppression.

Social control also operates through various discourses that legitimise certain types of crowd behaviour and delegitimise others. Although discourses such as "peaceful protest" should be seen as productive and positive, it is important that crowd members consider how the discursive and material practices permitted by these discourses might limit their ability to bring about political change by means of crowd action.

All crowd events require planning, establishing ground rules and norms, self-organisation, task allocation and liaising with authorities to varying degrees. Crowd members should consider the ways in which, by taking part in these self-regulatory processes, they may become subject to technologies of social control, reproducing the very oppressive practices that they attempt to challenge.

4.2. Evaluation and implications

Willig (2008) argued that this type of qualitative research, with constructionist epistemology, should not be evaluated based on the criteria of reliability and generalisability which are applied to positivist research. She also argued that the validity of Foucauldian research should be evaluated within a discursive framework that conceptualises the researcher as authoring rather than discovering knowledge. Thus, this study should be viewed as a discursive construction produced by the researcher and not as an exhaustive account of the data obtained from participants. Therefore, this study attempted to present the analysis in a way as transparent as possible by providing a detailed description of the analytic steps, and including extracts from the participants' interviews and references to the wider literature within the text to allow readers the opportunity to evaluate the validity of the analysis themselves.

For ethical reasons, this study recruited participants who live in the UK; specifically, young post-graduate students from middle class backgrounds. However, it would be interesting to conduct similar studies that recruit participants from different social and cultural backgrounds to allow a comparison of the ways in which social class and culture operate to enable and restrict subjectivities and social actions in crowds.

This study proposed that drawing on the concept of governmentality and the values of the neoliberal agenda is suitable to analyse the talk of Egyptian participants who have been heavily influenced by Western values. However, one might take a post-colonialist perspective and argue that using a Western-oriented framework to investigate crowd activity within a non-Western context distorts and limits our understanding of these societies (Said, 1978) and silences the voices of those who are marginalised by the dominant Western culture (Spivak, 1988). Furthermore, Jeffreys (2009) proposed that the notion of governmentality in non-Western societies is not based on values of freedom and liberty as in the Western tradition but on distinct values that characterise these societies. For example, he argued that governmentality in China is based on rational approaches to organisation and administration. This argument highlights the need for future research on the approaches to governance in non-Western contexts as well as the subjectivities and social actions enabled by them.

This study explored the ways in which the crowd was constructed by crowd members themselves. However, it would be interesting to conduct similar studies that investigate crowd action from the perspectives of the media, the police officers who control crowd activity and citizens who did not participate in or opposed the Tahrir Square sit-in to explore a wider range of constructions of the crowd in Egyptian society. Another issue for future research that this study raises is how the techniques of social control that aim to maintain the status quo operate through crowd self-regulatory practices and various discourses such as "peace" and "civility" that define legitimate crowd activities.

Finally, this study sought to approach crowd activity from the perspective of crowd members in a way that challenges the dominant accounts of the crowd and highlights the risks as well as the opportunities for resisting oppression and bringing on political change entailed in crowd action. It is hoped that this type of research could be viewed as opening up critical approaches to understand crowds, alternative ways of being and possibilities for collective actions that liberate those who are oppressed and marginalised. As Foucault (1989: pp. 305-306) states:

> "The work of an intellectual is not to mould the political will of others; it is, through the analyses that he does in his own field, to re-examine evidence and assumptions, to shake up habitual ways of working and thinking, to dissipate conventional familiarities, to re-evaluate rules and institutions and to participate in the formation of a political will (where he has his role as citizen to play)".

References

Allport, F. H. (1924). *Social psychology*. New York: Houghton Mifflin.

Ammar, A. (2007). Role of leadership in disaster management and crowd control. *Prehospital & Disaster Medicine*, *22*(6), 527-528.

Arribas-Ayllon, M., & Walkerdine, V. (2008). Foucauldian Discourse Analysis. In C. Willig & W. Stainton-Rogers (Eds.), *The Sage handbook of qualitative research in psychology* (pp. 91-108). London: Sage.

Bendersky, J.W. (2007). "Panic": The impact of Le Bon's crowd Psychology on U.S. military thought. *Journal of the History of the Behavioral Sciences*, *43*, 257-283.

Burgress-limerick, T., & Burgress-limerick, R. (1998). Conversational Interviews and Multi-case Researcher in Psychology. *Australian Journal of Psychology*, *50*(2), 63-70.

Burr, V. (1995). *An Introduction to Social Constructionism*. London: Routledge.

Caldwell, A. (2012). *Trickle down this effect: negotiations of culture, care, and freedom in contemporary Cairo international schools* (MA thesis, American University, Cairo). Retrieved from http://dar.aucegypt.edu/handle/10526/3160

Colman, A.M. (1991). Crowd Psychology in South African murder trails. *American Psychologist, 46*(10), 1071-1079.

Cronin, P., & Reicher, S. (2006). A study of the factors that influence how senior officers police crowd events: on SIDE outside the laboratory. *British Journal of Social Psychology*, 45, 175-196.

Diener, E. (1979). Deindividuation, self awareness and disinhibition. *Journal of Personality and Social Psychology, 37*, 1160-1171.

Doosje, B., Spears, R., & Ellemers, N. (2002). Social identity as both cause and effect: The development of group identification in response to anticipated and actual changes in intergroup status hierarchy. *British Journal of Social Psychology, 39*, 579- 604.

Drury, J. (2002). When the mobs are looking for witches to burn
nobody's safe: Talking about the reactionary crowd. *Discourse
and Society*, *13*, 41-72.

Drury, J., & Reicher, S. (1999). The intergroup dynamics of collective
empowerment: Substantiating the social identity model of crowd
behaviour. *Group Processes and Intergroup Relations, 2*, 231-
402.

Drury, J., & Reicher, S. (2000). Collective action and psychological
change: The emergence of new social identities. *British Journal
of Social Psychology*, 39, 579-604.

Drury, J., & Reicher, S. (2005). Explaining enduring empowerment: A
comparative study of collective action and psychological
outcomes. *European Journal of Social Psychology*, 35, 35-58.

Drury, J., & Winter, G. (2003). Social Identity as a source of strength in
mass emergencies and other crowd events. *International Journal
of Mental Health*, *32*(4), 77-93.

Drury, J., Cocking, C., & Reicher, S. (2009). Everyone for
    themselves? A comparative study of crowd solidarity among
    emergency survivors. *British Journal of Social Psychology*,
    48(3), 487-506.

Durrheim, K., & Foster, D. (1999). Technologies of social control:
    crowd management in liberal democracy. *Economy and Society*,
    28, 56-74.

Festinger, L., Pepitone, A., & Newcomb, T. (1952). Some
    consequences of deindividuation in a group. *Journal of
    Abnormal and Social Psychology*, *47*, 382-389.

Finlay, L. (2002). Negotiating the swamp: the opportunity and
    challenge of reflectivity and research practice. *Qualitative
    research, 2*(2), 209-230.

Fornaciari, F. (2012). Framing the Egyptian Revolution: A content
analysis of Al Jazeera English and the BBC. *Journal of Arab &
Muslim Media Research*, 4, 223-235.

Foucault, M. (1972). *The Archaeology of knowledge.* London:
Tavistock.

Foucault, M. (1977). *Discipline and Punish: the Birth of the Prison.*
Cornwall: Penguin.

Foucault, M. (1982). The Subject and Power. *Critical Inquiry*, *8*(4),
777-795.

Foucault, M. (1988). 'Technologies of the Self'. In L.H.Martin , H.
Gutman & P.H. Hutton (Eds.), *Technologies of the Self: A
Seminar with Michel Foucault, October 25, 1982* (pp. 16-49).
Amherst: The University of Massachusetts Press.

Foucault, M. (1989). The concern for truth. In S. Lotringer (Ed.),
Foucault Live: *Interviews,* 1966-84 (pp. 293-308). New York:
Semiotext.

Foucault, M. (1990). *The History of sexuality: an introduction.* New York: Vintage Books.

Foucault, M. (1994). Life: experience and science. In J. D. Faubion (Ed.), *Essential works of Foucault 1954-1984. Volume two: aesthetics, method and epistemology* (pp. 465-478). London: Penguin Books.

Freud, S. (1900). *The Interpretation of Dreams.* Pengiun Freud Library, volume 4. London: Pengiun.

Graumann, C., & Moscovici, S. (1996). *Changing conceptions of crowd mind and behaviour.* New York: Springer-Verlag.

Hardt, M., & Negri, A. (2009). *Commonwealth.* Cambridge, MA: Harvard University Press/ Belknap Press.

Harper, D. (1995). Discourse Analysis and 'Mental Health'. *Journal of Mental Health, 4*, 347-357.

Harris, S. (2010). *Development through Faith: The Ma'adi Life Makers and the Islamic Entrepreneurial Subject* (MA thesis,

Georgetown University, Washington). Retrieved from
http://hdl.handle.net/1961/5898

Ismail, S. (2011). Authoritarian Government, Neoliberalism and
Everyday Civilities in Egypt. *Third World Quarterly*, *32*(5),
845-862.

Jeffreys, E. (2009). *China's Governmentalities: governing change,
changing government*. New York: Routledge.

Joya, A. (2011). The Egyptian revolution: crisis of neoliberalism and
the potential for democratic politics. *Review of African
Economy*. *129*, 367- 386.

Khamis, S. (2011). The Transformative Egyptian Media Landscape:
Changes, Challenges and Comparative Perspectives.
International Journal of Communication, *5*, 1159-1177.

Kvale, S. (1996). *An Introduction to Qualitative Interviewing*.
California: Sage.

Le Bon, G. (1895, trans. 1947). *The Crowd: A Study of the Popular Mind*. London: Ernest Benn.

Marques, O. (2010). Choice-Makers and Risk-Takers in Neo-Liberal Liquid Modernity: The Contradiction of the "Entrepreneurial" Sex Worker. *International Journal of Criminology and Sociological Theory*, *3*(1), 314-332.

McNay, L. (2009). Self as enterprise: Dilemmas of control and resistance in Foucault's The Birth of Biopolitics. *Theory & Culture, 26*(6), 55-77.

McPhail, C. (1991). *The Myth of the Madding Crowd*. New York: Aldine de Gruyter.

Middlemist, R.D., Knowles, E.S., & Matter, C.F. (1976). Personal invasions in the lavatory: Suggestive evidence for arousal. *Journal of Personality and Social Psychology*, *33*, 541-546.

Moscovici, S., & Nemeth, C. (1974). *Social psychology: Classic and contemporary integrations*. Oxford: Rand McNally.

Nye, R. (1975). *The Origins of Crowd Psychology*. London: Sage.

Parker, I. (2005). *Qualitative Psychology. Introducing Radical Research*. Maidenhead: Open University Press.

Parker, I. (1992). *Discourse Dynamics: Critical Analysis for Social and Individual Psychology*. London: Routledge.

Postmes, T., & Spears, R. (1998). Deindividuation and ant-normative behaviour: A meta-analysis. *Psychological Bulletin*, *123*, 238-259.

Reicher, S., & Potter, J. (1985). Psychological theory as intergroup perspective: a comparative: a comparative analysis of 'scientific' and 'lay' accounts' of crowd events. *Human Relations*, *38*, 167-189.

Reicher, S. D. (1987). Crowd behaviour as a social action. In J.C. Turner (Ed.), *Rediscovering the social group: a self Categorisation theory* (pp.171- 202). Oxford: Blackwell.

Reicher, S. D. (1997). Collective psychology and the psychology of the self. *BPS Social Section Newsletter, 36,* 3-15.

Reicher, S. D. (2001). The psychology of crowd dynamics. In M. Hogg & R.S. Tindale (Eds.), *The Blackwell handbook of social psychology: Group processes* (pp.182-208). Oxford: Blackwell.

Reicher, S. D. (1996). 'The Battle of Westminster': Developing the social identity model of crowd behaviour in order to explain the initiation and development of collective conflict. *European Journal of Social Psychology, 26,* 115-34.

Reicher, S.D. (1984). The St Paul's riot: An explanation of the limits of crowd action in terms of a social identity model. *European Journal of Social Psychology, 14,* 1-21.

Rose, N. (1999). *Governing the soul: The shaping of the private self* (2nd ed.). London: Free Association Books.

Said, E. (1978). *Orientalism.* London: Routledge and Kegan Paul.

Schindler, A. (2012). *Visualising the unfamiliar: ethnography of an emerging moment in Cairo* (MA thesis, American University, Cairo). Retrieved from http://dar.aucegypt.edu/bitstream/handle/10526/3117/Visualizing%20the%20Unfamiliar-%20Ethnography%20of%20an%20Emerging%20Moment%20in%20Cairo.pdf?sequence=1

Schweingruber, D., & Wohltstein, R. T. (2005). The madding crowd goes to school: Myth about crowds on introductory sociology books. *Teaching Psychology*, *33*, 136-153.

Singer, J.E., Brush, C.E., & Lublin, S.C. (1965). Some aspects of dindividuation: Identification and conformity. *Journal of Experimental Social Psychology*, *1*, 356-378.

Smart, C., & Smart, B. (1978). *Women, Sexuality and Social Control*. London: Routledge & Kegan Paul.

Spivak, G. (1988). Can the subaltern speak? In C. Nelson, & L. Grossberg (Eds.), *Marxism and the interpretation of culture* (pp. 217-313). London: Macmillan.

Stott, C., Hutchison, P., & Drury, J. (2001). 'Hooligans' abroad? Inter-group dynamics, social identity and participation in collective 'disorder' at the 1998 World Cup Finals. *British Journal of Social Psychology*, *40*(3), 359-384.

Turner, J.C., Oakes, P.J., Haslam, S.J., & McGarty, C. (1994). Self and collective: Cognition and social context. *Personality and Social Psychology Bulletin, 20,* 454-63.

Turner, R. H., & Killian, L.M. (1987). *Collective behaviour*. Englewood Cliffs, NJ: Prentice-Hall.

Van Zomeren, M., & Spears, R. (2011). The Crowd as psychological cue to in-group support for collective action against collective disadvantage. *Contemporary Social Science*, *6*(3), 325-341.

Vider, S. (2004). Rethinking Crowd Violence: Self-Categorization Theory and the Woodstock 1999 Riot. *Journal for the Theory of Social Behaviour*, *34*(2), 141-166.

Willig, C. (2008). *Introducing Qualitative Research In Psychology: Adventures In Theory And Method* (2nd ed.). Buckingham: Open University Press.

Printed in Germany
by Amazon Distribution
GmbH, Leipzig